Let's Talk About the Affair

Courageous Conversations for Life After Infidelity

Jeffrey D. Murrah

Restore The Family Press

Contents

Introduction

I f you're reading this book, you or your spouse has likely had an affair that has left your marriage reeling. You may feel a whirlwind of emotions—hurt, anger, betrayal, confusion, and despair. You might be questioning whether there's any hope for your relationship, wondering if you can ever move past this devastating betrayal.

As a counselor who has worked with countless couples in the aftermath of infidelity, I want to assure you that there is hope. I've witnessed marriages that seemed irreparably broken be restored and even thrive after an affair. However, the path to healing requires both partners to be willing to invest time and effort into self-reflection, honest communication, and rebuilding trust.

Throughout my years in practice, I've seen incredible transformation in couples like Madison and Ethan. When they first came to me, their marriage was hanging by a thread in the wake of Ethan's affair. The pain seemed insurmountable, and they had no idea how to talk to each other without causing more damage. They weren't even sure what to talk about. But with dedication, hard work, and a commitment to the principles you'll learn in this book, they slowly found their way back to each other. Today, their relationship is stronger than ever, characterized by genuine intimacy, trust, and happiness.

I share their story to offer you a beacon of hope, no matter how bleak your situation may appear right now. Your marriage is worth fighting for, and this book is designed to be a valuable tool in that fight. In these pages, you'll gain:

- Understanding of what led to the affair and the underlying issues in your marriage

- Strategies for managing your emotions so you can communicate effectively

- Practical techniques for initiating open, honest dialogue with your partner

- A step-by-step guide to rebuilding intimacy and trust

- Inspiring real-life stories of couples who have overcome infidelity

Whether you're the betrayed spouse reeling from the shock of discovery or the unfaithful partner desperate to make amends, this book is for you. While I can't guarantee the journey will be easy, I can tell you from professional experience that it will be worth it.

You may think, "How can I trust this book will work for us?" The truth is, the survival of your marriage depends on your capacity and willingness to re-establish communication and genuine connection with each other. By opening this book, you're already taking a brave step in that direction.

To make the most of this resource, I recommend:

1. Approach it with an open mind and heart, be receptive to new ideas, and take ownership of your role in the relationship.

2. Take your time to work through the material, carefully read each chapter, and complete the exercises. Create a manageable reading schedule that allows you to absorb the content at a pace that feels comfortable for you. Remember, healing is a process, and moving forward at a rhythm that works for your unique situation

is essential.

3. If possible, read the book with your spouse and share your thoughts and breakthroughs along the way. Set aside dedicated time for discussion and practice active listening to ensure both of you feel heard and understood. Consider using the reflection questions at the end of each chapter as prompts for deeper conversation and connection.

4. Seek additional support through therapy or support groups as you navigate the challenging road of affair recovery. A qualified therapist specializing in affair recovery can provide personalized guidance and support tailored to your specific needs. Don't hesitate to reach out for professional help when needed, as it can be an invaluable complement to your work through this book.

5. Revisit the material as needed. As you progress through your healing journey, you may find that different chapters or strategies become more relevant at different times. Don't hesitate to return to previous sections or re-read the book entirely as your needs and insights evolve.

6. Be patient and extend grace to yourself and your partner. Healing takes time, and setbacks are a normal part of the process. Prioritize self-care throughout your recovery journey and find practical ways to nurture your emotional well-being, such as engaging in hobbies, spending time in nature, or practicing mindfulness.

This book is a tool to support you on your path to healing. Over time, your wisdom and intuition will increase. With those improvements, you will use the material in a way that feels more authentic and helpful for your unique situation. The journey ahead may be challenging, but by committing to the process and taking it one step at a time, you can rebuild a stronger, more resilient relationship.

As you embark on this journey, know that change is possible. Healing can happen. Your marriage can emerge stronger on the other side of this crisis. All it takes is a willingness to start the conversation, one brave step at a time. Let's begin.

Laying the Foundation

Part One

Restore The Family Press

Chapter One

Understanding Affairs and Their Impact on Marriage

The discovery of an affair is a devastating blow to any marriage. In an instant, the trust, love, and commitment that form the bedrock of your relationship are called into question. You may feel like the rug has been ripped out from under you, leaving you disoriented, heartbroken, and unsure of where to turn.

If you're in this painful place, know you're not alone. Studies suggest that infidelity occurs in up to 40% of marriages, with both men and women being almost equally likely to stray.

While this statistic offers little comfort, it underscores an important truth: affairs are a common challenge many couples face. It means that countless others have walked this difficult path before you and have found their way to healing and renewal.

As you embark on your own journey of recovery, it's crucial to understand the complex factors that contribute to affairs. Rarely are they just about sexual attraction or a fleeting moment of weakness. More often, affairs arise from a tangled web of unmet needs, communication breakdowns, and emotional disconnection within the primary relationship. Affairs are often one spouse's solution to another problem.

Consider the story of Olivia and Roberto. From the outside, their marriage looked picture-perfect – a beautiful home, successful careers, and two adorable children. But behind closed doors, Olivia felt increasingly lonely and unseen. Consumed by work stress and family obligations, Roberto had become distant and emotionally unavailable. When a charming coworker began showering Olivia with attention and validation, she was drawn into an affair almost before she realized what was happening. She was drawn to the attention, craving it more with each interaction. Finally, she felt seen and alive.

Olivia's story highlights a common theme in many affairs: the longing for connection and intimacy. When we feel disconnected from our partner, when our emotional needs go unmet, we become vulnerable to seeking fulfillment elsewhere. This is not to excuse the choice to cheat but rather to understand the psychological underpinnings that can leave a relationship susceptible to infidelity.

As you grapple with the pain of betrayal, it's essential to remember that an affair does not reflect your worth as a partner or a person. The decision to stray is a choice made by the unfaithful spouse, and they must take full responsibility for the damage it causes. Their choice is about their value on you, NOT about your value as a whole. Blaming yourself, obsessing over what you could have done differently, or comparing yourself to the affair partner will only keep you stuck in a cycle of shame and self-doubt.

Instead, focus on what you need to begin the healing process. For many, this starts with a commitment to open, honest communication. Affairs thrive in secrecy, so shining a light on what happened is a crucial first step. This doesn't mean rehashing every painful detail but rather creating a safe space to express your feelings, ask questions, and begin to understand what led to the breakdown of your relationship.

It's also important to prioritize self-care during this time. When your world has been turned upside down, it's easy to neglect your own needs. But taking care of yourself – physically, emotionally, and spiritually – is not a luxury; it's a necessity. Whether it's leaning on the support of trusted friends and family, engaging in activities that bring you joy, or seeking the guidance of a therapist, do whatever you need to nurture yourself through this difficult chapter. This includes eating healthy. Although you may have lost your appetite, maintaining healthy nutrition is critical for your mental and emotional health.

As you move forward, remember there will be good days and bad days, moments of hope and moments of despair. Be patient with yourself and your partner as you navigate this uncharted territory. With time, commitment, and a willingness to grow, you can begin to rebuild your relationship on a foundation of renewed trust, intimacy, and understanding.

In the coming chapters, we'll explore practical strategies for communicating effectively, processing the complex emotions of betrayal, and gradually restoring trust. While the road ahead may be daunting, know you have the strength and resilience to weather this storm. By facing the pain head-on and doing the hard work of recovery, you open the door to a future of deeper love, greater wisdom, and profound personal growth.

Reflection Questions:

1. What unmet needs or feelings of disconnection may have left my marriage vulnerable to an affair?

2. How can I prioritize self-care and seek the support I need during this challenging time?

3. What steps can I take to create a safe space for open, honest communication with my partner as we begin the healing process? Safe space includes being able to talk to each other without interruptions, without threats, and without raised voices.

Chapter Two

Hurt People Hurt People

"Truth always carries with it confrontation. Truth demands confrontation; loving confrontation nevertheless." Francis Schaeffer

In the aftermath of an affair, it's easy to get caught up in a cycle of blame, anger, and resentment. You may find yourself lashing out at your partner, consumed by the need to make them feel the depth of your pain. Or you might turn that anger inward, berating yourself for not seeing the signs or being "enough" to keep your spouse from straying.

While these reactions are understandable, it's important to recognize that they rarely lead to healing or resolution. They often perpetuate a destructive cycle of hurt, where wounded partners unintentionally inflict more pain on each other and themselves.

The simple truth is that "hurt people hurt people." When we're in pain, it's natural to want to protect ourselves by striking out or withdrawing. When you are hurt, you may want to make your spouse hurt as badly as you do. But when we're not mindful of how our hurt drives our behavior, we risk causing further damage to our relationships and impeding our healing.

Consider the story of Rachel and David. When Rachel discovered that David had been having an emotional affair with a neighbor, she was devastated. She felt betrayed, humiliated, and consumed by a rage she had never known before. In her pain, Rachel began lashing out at David at every opportunity – belittling him in front of their children, airing his dirty laundry to their shared friends, and even threatening to get him fired from his job. She even entertained putting a sign in the front yard exposing his affair.

Rachel's parents divorced when she was young. She remembered that pain and was determined to keep her children from going through the heartache she endured as a child.

While Rachel's anger was justified, her hurtful actions only further drove David away and deepened their rift. It wasn't until Rachel began working with a therapist that she realized how her unresolved pain from a past betrayal was fueling her destructive behavior. By learning to process her hurt in healthier ways, Rachel was able to break the cycle of lashing out and start working toward genuine healing.

Rachel's story illustrates an important point: our pain doesn't exist in a vacuum. The wounds we carry from our past, whether from childhood traumas, previous relationships, or even societal messages about our worth and lovability, can profoundly shape how we react to betrayal in the present.

This is why one of the most crucial steps in affair recovery is doing your inner work. Before you can begin to repair your relationship, you must first tend to your emotional wounds. This means creating space to feel your feelings without judgment, learning healthy coping strategies, and seeking support from trusted friends, family members, or a qualified therapist.

It also means practicing self-compassion. When you're in the throes of betrayal trauma, it's easy to be harsh and unforgiving with yourself. You might berate yourself for not seeing the signs, blame yourself for your partner's choices, or feel like a failure for being unable to "get over it" quickly enough. But beating yourself up only compounds your pain and keeps you stuck in a negative spiral.

Instead, try to extend yourself the same grace and understanding you would offer a dear friend in a similar situation. Remind yourself that healing is not a linear process and that it's okay to have setbacks and bad days. Remind yourself that you are not a robot who merely executes the commands it is given. Treat yourself with kindness, prioritize your self-care, and trust that you will find your way through this difficult chapter with time and support.

As you begin to process your hurt in healthier ways, you'll be better equipped to approach your relationship from a place of clarity and groundedness. You'll be able to communicate your needs and boundaries more effectively, listen to your partner with greater empathy and patience, and make decisions about the future of your marriage from a place of strength rather than reactivity.

Healing from infidelity is a deeply personal journey, and there is no one-size-fits-all timeline or approach. Honor your unique process, and don't hesitate to seek the resources and support you need. Tending to your wounds with compassion and care lays the groundwork for genuine, lasting healing – for yourself and your relationship.

Reflection Questions:

1. How might my past experiences or unresolved hurts influence my reactions to my partner's betrayal? Consider whether you have ever felt similar pains in the past. If so, what happened that triggered those reactions?

2. What healthy coping strategies can I adopt to process my pain in constructive ways?

3. How can I practice self-compassion and prioritize my healing during this challenging time?

4. What does a healthy version of me look like?

Chapter Three

Developing a Growth Mindset

"Great works are performed, not by strength, but by perseverance." Samuel Johnson

When you're in the midst of the pain and chaos of infidelity, it can be hard to imagine a future where your marriage feels whole and happy again. You may be stuck in a spiral of negative thoughts, convinced that your relationship is damaged beyond repair or that you'll never be able to trust your partner again.

While these fears are understandable, they can become self-fulfilling prophecies if left unchecked. Statements like "He'll never change," "There's no hope," "There's no way in hell I'll ever forgive her," or "Once a cheater, always a cheater" program your mind in a negative direction. How we think about our challenges and capacity for change plays a significant role in our ability to heal and grow. This is where cultivating a growth mindset comes in.

Renowned psychologist Carol Dweck coined the term "growth mindset" to describe the belief that our abilities and relationships are not fixed but can be developed and strengthened through effort, learning, and perseverance. In contrast, a "fixed mindset" assumes that our qualities are carved in stone—that we're either inherently good at something or we're not, that our relationships either work or they don't.

When it comes to affair recovery, a fixed mindset might sound like: "I'll never be able to forgive them," "Our marriage is too broken to fix," or "I'm just not strong enough to get through this." These beliefs can quickly become paralyzing, keeping us stuck in a cycle of hopelessness and despair. They act as blinders, keeping you from seeing beyond the pain.

On the other hand, a growth mindset embraces the idea that change is possible – even in the darkest times. It sounds like: "This is incredibly hard, but I trust in my resilience," "We can rebuild our relationship," or "I'm committed to learning and growing from this experience."

There is a reason why communities struck by disasters often respond by rallying around a mantra of how strong the community is. This mindset helps them by giving them hope and developing resilience.

Take the story of Sarah and Mike. When Sarah first learned of Mike's infidelity, she was certain it was the end of their marriage. She couldn't fathom ever being able to trust him again, let alone forgive him for shattering their life together. She spent weeks oscillating between rage, despair, and utter exhaustion, convinced that she would live the rest of her life under the shadow of betrayal.

It wasn't until Sarah began working with a skilled therapist that she started to shift her perspective. Her therapist introduced her to the concept of a growth mindset and encouraged her to question some of her fixed beliefs about herself, Mike, and their relationship. Slowly but surely, Sarah began to open up to the idea that healing was possible – that she and Mike could learn from this crisis and use it as a catalyst for deeper intimacy and understanding.

This shift didn't happen overnight, and it certainly wasn't easy. There were many days when Sarah slipped back into hopelessness and despair. She felt like a ping-pong ball bouncing back and forth from hopeful to hopeless, even several times a day. But by consistently choosing to reframe her thoughts and focus on small, incremental changes, she began cultivating a greater sense of resilience and hope.

Developing a growth mindset in the face of infidelity requires patience, self-compassion, and a willingness to step outside your comfort zone. It means being open to new ideas, perspectives, and approaches, even when they initially feel foreign or uncomfortable. It means embracing the idea that struggle and setbacks are not signs of failure but rather opportunities for learning and growth.

One powerful way to cultivate a growth mindset is through the practice of reframing. When you find yourself stuck in a negative thought loop, take a step back and ask yourself: "Is there another way to look at this situation? What can I learn from this experience? How might facing this challenge help me grow and develop in the long run?"

It's also important to surround yourself with people who support and encourage a growth mindset. This might mean seeking out a therapist or coach who can help you reframe your thoughts and beliefs, joining a support group of others committed to personal development, or even just curating your social media feed to include more uplifting and growth-oriented content.

Adopting a growth mindset doesn't mean denying the very real pain and challenges of infidelity. It's not about "thinking positive" or forcing yourself to forgive and move on before you're ready. Rather, it's about creating space for the possibility of healing and transformation, even in great hardship.

You open yourself to new possibilities and pathways by embracing a growth mindset. You begin to see challenges as opportunities for learning and development rather than insurmountable roadblocks. Most importantly, you tap into your innate resilience and strength, trusting your capacity to weather even the toughest storms.

Reflection Questions:

1. What fixed beliefs do I hold about myself, my partner, or our relationship that might be keeping me stuck?

2. How can I practice reframing negative thoughts and embracing a more growth-oriented perspective?

3. What resources or support systems can I seek out to help me cultivate a growth mindset during this challenging time?

4. What do my negative thoughts say about me and my own needs?

Opening Up Communication

Part Two

Restore The Family Press

Chapter Four

Questions that Shut Down vs Open Up

Effective communication is the foundation of any healthy relationship, but it becomes especially crucial after an affair. As you and your partner navigate the rocky terrain of betrayal, how you talk to each other can open up new pathways to healing or deepen the wounds even further.

One of the most powerful tools in your communication toolkit is the art of asking questions. The right questions can create a space for honesty, vulnerability, and connection, while the wrong ones can shut down dialogue and leave both partners feeling attacked or defensive.

Let's consider the case of Amanda and Tom. When Amanda first discovered Tom's affair, she was consumed by a whirlwind of unanswered questions. Why did he do it? How could he betray her trust like this? What did she do wrong? In her desperation for answers, Amanda would often bombard Tom with accusatory questions the moment he walked in the door. "Why did you cheat on me? Don't you love me anymore? How could you be so selfish?"

While Amanda's questions were understandable, given the depth of her pain, they rarely led to the honest, healing conversations she craved. Instead, Tom would either shut down completely or respond with defensiveness and anger. It wasn't until Amanda learned to reframe her questions in a more open-ended, non-judgmental way that they could start having more productive dialogues.

In the early stages of affair recovery, it's common to have many questions swirling in your mind. You may be desperate to understand why the affair happened, what it meant, and how you can ever trust your partner again. These are all valid concerns, but bombarding your partner with an interrogation-style barrage of questions rarely leads to the answers or the healing you seek.

It's important to be mindful of the types of questions you ask and how you ask them. Questions that start with "why," for example, can often feel like an accusation or an attack, putting your partner on the defensive. "Why did you cheat on me?" "Why wasn't I enough for you?" "Why did you lie to me?" While these questions may burn in your mind, they rarely lead to productive dialogue. Such questions can damage your communication with your spouse. When you ask such questions of yourself, they can also produce damaging results as well.

"What" and "how" questions, on the other hand, tend to open up more space for reflection and dialogue. "What was going on for you that led to the affair?" "How can we rebuild trust moving forward?" "What do you need from me to feel safe and supported in our relationship?" These types of questions invite your partner to share their perspective without feeling blamed or shamed. They create a way to move forward.

Another couple, Emily and Jason, found that shifting to "what" and "how" questions was a turning point in their healing process. Instead of asking, "Why did you do this to me?" Emily asked Jason, "What was missing in our relationship that made you weak about having an affair?" Instead of demanding, "How could you be so heartless?" she asked, "How are you feeling about what happened, and what do you need from me to rebuild trust?" By inviting Jason to share his perspective without judgment, Emily could better understand the factors that contributed to the affair and what they both needed to heal.

Avoiding loaded or multiple-choice questions that presume a certain answer is also important. For example, "Did you cheat on me because you're selfish or because you just don't love me anymore?" This type of question puts your partner in a no-win situation and is more likely to escalate tension than promote understanding. It also creates false options. The question looks like there are options, yet in reality, it amounts to choosing between two pre-determined answers.

Instead, ask open-ended questions that allow your partner to share their thoughts and feelings. "Can you help me understand what was happening to you then?" "What did the affair represent for you?" "How are you feeling about our relationship now?" These types of questions demonstrate a genuine desire to understand your partner's perspective, even though you don't agree with their actions.

It's also crucial to be mindful of your state of mind when engaging in these conversations. If you're feeling overwhelmed by anger, betrayal, or despair, it may not be the right time to dive into a deep discussion. Take time to process your own emotions first, whether through journaling, speaking with a trusted friend, or working with a therapist. You'll be better equipped to approach the conversation with curiosity and openness when you're in a more grounded place.

As you practice asking more open-ended, non-judgmental questions, be prepared for answers that may be difficult to hear. Your partner's perspective on the affair may be very different from your own, and it may challenge your assumptions about your relationship or even yourself. Try to listen with an open mind, even if you disagree with what they're saying. The goal is not to agree with everything but rather to truly understand each other's experiences and perspectives.

Effective communication is a two-way street. As much as you may want answers and explanations from your partner, they likely have their questions and concerns. Be willing to share your thoughts and feelings, even when they feel vulnerable or uncomfortable. The more you can show up with honesty and openness, the more you create a foundation for genuine healing.

Of course, there may be times when communication breaks down despite your best efforts. Old wounds get triggered, defenses go up, and you find yourselves stuck in a painful cycle of blame and reactivity. When this happens, don't hesitate to seek outside support. A skilled couples therapist can help you navigate these difficult conversations and provide tools for communicating more effectively.

With practice and patience, you can learn to ask questions that invite connection and understanding rather than shutting each other down. It takes time to change your thinking and the kinds of questions you ask.

It is also important to be genuine in your use of questions. This amounts to genuinely seeking their answers rather than having your spouse answer multiple-choice questions you already selected for them. By approaching your partner with genuine curiosity, empathy, and a willingness to listen, you begin to create a new foundation of trust and intimacy—one conversation at a time.

Reflection Questions:

1. What types of questions do I tend to ask when I'm feeling hurt or triggered? How might I reframe these questions to be more open-ended and non-judgmental?

2. How can I create space to process my own emotions before diving into difficult conversations with my partner?

3. What support systems can I lean on to help me navigate the challenges of communicating in the aftermath of an affair?

4. How can you show genuine interest in their answers rather than having a 'gotcha' kind of attitude?

Chapter Five

Creating Emotional Safety

In the aftermath of an affair, one of the most crucial elements for healing is creating a sense of emotional safety within your relationship. When trust has been shattered, and emotions are running high, it can feel like every conversation is a minefield littered with triggers and potential explosions.

Take the example of Sarah and Michael. In the early days of navigating Michael's infidelity, Sarah found herself constantly on edge, bracing for the next painful revelation or argument. Even well-meaning questions from Michael, like "How are you doing today?" felt loaded with hidden accusations and judgments. Sarah struggled to express her feelings without lashing out at him or shutting down completely.

However, to truly heal and move forward, Sarah and Michael needed to learn how to communicate openly and honestly about what happened, how they felt, and what they needed from each other going forward. They needed a place to talk without fighting. This required a foundation of emotional safety - a shared understanding that they could express themselves without fear of judgment, blame, or retaliation.

Building this kind of safety is easier said than done, especially in the early stages of affair recovery. Your nerves are raw, your defenses are up, and the slightest misstep can send you spiraling back into pain and reactivity. But with patience, commitment, and a few key strategies, you can create a space where you and your partner feel seen, heard, and supported.

One of the first steps in creating emotional safety is to set clear boundaries and ground rules for your conversations. This might include things like agreeing to take breaks when emotions run high, committing to avoid name-calling or blaming language, or establishing a safe word that either of you can use when you need to pause or redirect the conversation. Safety is a paramount concern. If weapons are brandished or threats are made, it is time to stop the conversation for a while. Conversations about such hot emotional topics require physical safety. Genuine conversation can only occur where there is safety.

Another couple, Lisa and Mark, found that setting clear boundaries around their communication was a game-changer in their healing process. They agreed that if either of them felt overwhelmed or triggered during a conversation, they would say "pause" and take a 20-minute break to regroup. They also committed to avoiding generalizations or absolutes like "you always" or "you never," instead focusing on specific behaviors and their impact.

During these discussions, it's also important to be mindful of your tone and body language. Even if your words are neutral, a sharp tone or closed-off posture can convey that you're not open to hearing your partner's perspective. Making clenched fists or threatening gestures are also conversation killers. Try to approach each conversation with a spirit of curiosity and empathy, even when you disagree with what your partner is saying.

Another key aspect of emotional safety is learning to validate each other's experiences and emotions. Validation doesn't mean agreeing with everything your partner says or feels but rather acknowledging the underlying pain, fear, or frustration beneath their words. It's the difference between saying, "I can't believe you're still hung up on this," and "I can see how much this is hurting you, and I want to understand more."

Feeling validated by our partner sends the message that our feelings matter and that we're not alone in our struggles. It creates a sense of connection and partnership, even during great pain. Offering validation to our partner helps them feel seen and understood, which goes a long way in diffusing defensiveness and promoting open, honest dialogue.

Of course, creating emotional safety is not just about what happens during your conversations but also about the environment you create around them. This means being intentional about when, where, and how you engage in these discussions. Trying to have a deep, emotional conversation in the middle of a busy day or with distractions all around you is a recipe for frustration and disconnection.

Instead, try to carve out dedicated time and space for your healing work. This might mean setting aside a specific evening each week for a "check-in" conversation, going for a walk together in a peaceful setting, or even creating a special "talking stick" or other object that symbolizes your commitment to open, respectful communication. The more you can create a sense of sacred space around your conversations, the more likely you are to approach them with the care and attention they deserve.

Lisa and Mark found that creating a ritual around their conversations helped them approach the process with greater intention and care. Every Sunday evening, they would light a candle, sit down together, and take turns sharing their thoughts, feelings, and experiences from the week.

Having this dedicated time and space allowed them to focus fully on each other and their healing journey without the distractions of daily life.

It's also important to recognize that creating emotional safety is ongoing. There will be moments when, despite your best efforts, one or both of you will get triggered and fall back into old patterns of defensiveness, blame, or withdrawal. When this happens, it's crucial to have a plan in place for how to repair the rupture and reconnect with each other.

This might involve taking a break to cool down, offering a sincere apology for any hurtful words or actions, or finding a way to express your underlying fears and needs in a more vulnerable way. The key is approaching these moments with compassion and a commitment to growth rather than shame or self-judgment.

As you continue to practice these skills and strategies, you'll likely find that emotional safety becomes easier and more natural over time. You'll develop a shared language and understanding that allows you to navigate even the toughest conversations with grace and resilience. And you'll begin to experience the deep healing and connection that comes from truly showing up for each other, even in the darkest of times.

Creating emotional safety is not about perfection but rather about progress. It's about the willingness to show up, again and again, with an open heart and a commitment to growth. And it's about trusting that, even when the road gets bumpy, you have the strength and the tools to navigate it together.

Reflection Questions:

1. What boundaries or ground rules could we establish to create a greater sense of emotional safety in our conversations?

2. How can I practice validating my partner's experiences and emotions, even when I disagree with their perspective?

3. What rituals or practices could we put in place to create a sense of sacred space around our healing work?

Chapter Six

Speaking the Truth in Love

"..Speaking the truth in love.." Ephesians 4:15

There comes a time in recovery when you must have difficult, honest conversations with your partner. You may need to share your deepest feelings of hurt and betrayal, ask tough questions about the affair, or express your needs and boundaries moving forward. These conversations can be incredibly challenging, requiring a delicate balance of honesty and compassion, firmness and flexibility.

One helpful framework for navigating these discussions is the concept of "speaking the truth in love." This means communicating your truth—your thoughts, feelings, and experiences—directly and honestly in a spirit of love, respect, and a genuine desire for healing and connection. Going to either extreme, either truth without love or love without truth, is damaging.

Consider the case of Emily and David. After Emily discovered David's affair, she struggled to have productive conversations with him. Whenever she tried to express her hurt and anger, it came out as biting criticism and blame. "How could you do this to me? To our family? You're so selfish and irresponsible!" she would shout, leaving David feeling attacked and defensive.

It wasn't until Emily learned about the concept of speaking the truth in love that she could shift her approach. She began focusing on expressing her feelings and experiences rather than attacking David's character. "I feel so betrayed and devastated by your actions," she said during one conversation. "I'm struggling to understand how this could happen and what it means for our marriage. I need you to help me make sense of it all." By owning her truth and inviting David into a dialogue, Emily created more space for understanding and healing.

Speaking the truth in love is not about sugarcoating or avoiding difficult realities. It's not about giving them a piece of your mind, saying what you think your partner wants to hear, or hiding your pain and frustration. Rather, it's about finding a way to express your truth in a way that invites understanding, dialogue, and growth.

This can be a tricky balance to strike, especially when emotions are running high and triggers abound. It's all too easy to slip into blame, criticism, or defensiveness, even when you intend to be honest and authentic. So, how do you speak your truth in a way that promotes healing rather than more hurt?

One key is focusing on "I" statements rather than "you" statements. Instead of saying, "You ruined our marriage with your selfish choices," try something like, "I feel so betrayed and heartbroken by what happened, and I'm struggling to trust and feel safe in our relationship." Notice how the second statement expresses the same underlying truth but in a way that takes ownership of your feelings and experiences.

Another couple, Javier and Isabella, found that timing was crucial when it came to speaking their truth in love. Early in their healing process, Isabella often cornered corner Javier as soon as he walked in the door from work, desperate to talk about the affair. But Javier, already feeling stressed and overwhelmed, would instantly shut down or lash out in response.

Through couples therapy, Javier and Isabella learned to be more intentional about when and how they approached difficult conversations. They began to schedule dedicated time each week to check in with each other, creating a predictable, safe space to share their thoughts and feelings. They also practiced starting their conversations with an affirmation of their love and commitment, even during the struggle. "I know we're both hurting right now," Isabella might say, "but I want you to know I'm still in this with you. I'm here to listen and to work through this together."

As you share your truth, try to be specific and concrete. Instead of making sweeping generalizations or accusations, focus on specific behaviors, actions, or patterns you've observed and how they've impacted you. For example, instead of saying, "You never support me," try something like, "When I was sharing my feelings about the affair last night, and you walked out of the room, I felt so alone and dismissed. We must find a way to stay engaged and present with each other, even when things get tough."

It's also crucial to create space for your partner to share their truth and perspective, even if it's difficult to hear. Speaking the truth in love is not a one-way street but rather a dialogue in which both partners are invited to show up with honesty, vulnerability, and a willingness to listen and understand. You need to allow them to share uninterrupted. Their truth is also important to hear and understand.

This doesn't mean that you have to agree with everything your partner says or that their perspective negates your own experiences. They may not recall the facts the same way you do, yet it remains important to hear them out. It means approaching the conversation with a spirit of openness and a desire to truly hear and understand where they're coming from.

Of course, speaking the truth in love is not always easy, and there will likely be times when, despite your best efforts, the conversation goes off the rails. When this happens, it's important to have a plan in place for how to regroup and reconnect. This might involve taking a break to cool down, seeking the support of a therapist or mediator, or finding a way to collect your thoughts, feelings, and needs in writing rather than in the heat of the moment. Going in the right direction is more important than how fast you head there. Taking your time for breaks or to collect yourself is important.

As you continue on your healing journey, there will likely be many moments when you need to have brave, honest conversations with your partner. At times, that bravery consists of listening to your spouse without reacting. At other times, bravery consists of being able to say out loud what you have been feeling and thinking.

By approaching each conversation with a commitment to honesty, compassion, and growth, you can slowly but start rebuilding the trust and intimacy that have been lost.

Speaking the truth in love is about showing up with your whole heart and doing your best to create a safe, supportive space for healing and connection. It's about trusting that, even in the midst of great pain and uncertainty, the truth really can set you free - free to love, to heal, and to create the kind of relationship you both deserve.

Reflection Questions:

1. What are some of the hardest truths I need to share with my partner, and how might I express them in a way that is honest but also loving and respectful?

2. How can I prepare myself to allow my partner to share their truth and perspective, even when it's difficult for me to hear?

3. What practices or strategies can I implement to help me stay grounded and centered when difficult conversations start to feel overwhelming or triggering?

Chapter Seven

The Power of Writing

"Handle them carefully, for words have more power than atom bombs." -Pearl Strachan Hurd

When we think about affair recovery, we often focus on the importance of open, honest communication between partners. While having those face-to-face conversations is indeed crucial, there's another powerful tool that can profoundly support your healing journey: writing.

Writing has a way of unlocking our deepest thoughts and feelings, providing clarity and insight that can be hard to access through conversation alone. When we put pen to paper (or fingers to keyboard), we create a space for ourselves to process our experiences, explore our emotions, and gain a new perspective on our challenges and opportunities for growth.

Take the example of Lila and Sam. When Lila first discovered Sam's affair, she found herself overwhelmed by a tidal wave of emotions - rage, despair, confusion, and a deep sense of betrayal. She knew she needed to talk to Sam about what had happened, but every time she tried, she either exploded in anger or dissolved into tears.

Lila's therapist suggested that she try writing to process her feelings and clarify her thoughts. Although she was skeptical at first, she decided to try it. She started by free-writing for a few minutes each day, pouring out all the pain and chaos that was swirling inside her.

As the days passed, Lila found that her writing was starting to shift. She began to see patterns in her emotional reactions to understand the deeper fears and insecurities that were being triggered by Sam's betrayal. She also started recognizing glimmers of hope and resilience within herself - a core of strength she could draw upon as she navigated this difficult chapter.

Lila's writing also became a way for her to communicate with Sam in a more thoughtful, intentional way. When she felt ready, she talked to him, expressing her pain, questions, and hopes for their relationship. By organizing her thoughts on the page, she expressed herself in a way that felt clear, calm, and true to her heart.

(Note: Avoid writing a letter or email to your spouse. That is not the purpose of this exercise. Use the writing to organize your thoughts. Writing is not a replacement for genuine conversation.)

Another couple, Sophia and Lucas, found that writing became a powerful tool for rebuilding trust and intimacy after Lucas's affair. As part of their healing work, their therapist suggested that they start a shared journal where they could write to each other about their experiences, their feelings, and their hopes for the future.

At first, both Sophia and Lucas were hesitant. The idea of being so vulnerable with each other felt scary, especially in the context of the betrayal they were working through. Each was used to hiding what they felt from each other. But as they began to write, they found that the practice created a new space for honesty, empathy, and connection between them.

Through their shared writing, Sophia and Lucas could express things that felt too raw or scary to say out loud. They could take the time to hear and absorb each other's words without getting caught up in the reactivity of the moment. And they could start to rebuild a sense of safety and trust, one honest exchange at a time.

Of course, like any tool, writing is not a magic bullet. It's not a substitute for the hard work of talking to each other across the table, tackling the hard subjects, and behavior change. But it can be a powerful complement to these efforts, providing a space for deep reflection, self-discovery, and emotional processing.

If you're new to writing as a tool for healing, start small. Set aside a few minutes each day to jot down your thoughts and feelings without worrying about grammar, spelling, or coherence. You might start with a simple prompt, like "Today, I feel..." or "I'm struggling with..." and see where your writing takes you.

As you become more comfortable with the practice, you might try more structured exercises, like writing a letter to your partner or yourself from a place of compassion and understanding. These initial letters are not intended to be sent but rather to help you identify and organize your thoughts and feelings. You might also consider starting a shared journal with your partner, as Sophia and Lucas did, to foster greater intimacy and trust.

Remember, too, that your writing is entirely your own. You don't have to share it with anyone if you don't want to (although you may find it helpful to discuss some of your insights with your partner or a trusted friend). The point is not to create a polished piece of prose but rather to create a space for yourself to be authentic, vulnerable, and real.

Writing can be a powerful ally on your healing journey - a way to process your experiences, gain clarity and insight, and develop a more compassionate, resilient relationship with yourself and your partner. Making writing a regular part of your self-care practice opens the door to deeper self-awareness, emotional healing, and relational growth.

So grab a pen and a notebook, find a quiet spot where you feel safe and comfortable, and let the words flow. Trust that, with each page you fill, you take a brave and important step towards healing, wholeness, and a brighter future for yourself and your relationship.

Reflection Questions:

1. What are some of the thoughts, feelings, or experiences that I've been holding inside that I could explore through writing? If you can't find the words for it, can you draw a picture of it?

2. How might I use writing to practice self-compassion and develop a more supportive inner dialogue?

3. What kind of writing practice could I commit to as part of my self-care and healing journey (e.g., daily journaling, letter-writing, prompted exercises)?

Rebuilding Intimacy

Part Three

Restore The Family Press

Chapter Eight

Making Room for Each Other

In the aftermath of an affair, the very concept of intimacy can feel like a distant memory. The trust, vulnerability, and closeness that once defined your relationship may now seem shattered beyond repair. How do you even begin rebuilding a sense of connection when the foundation has been so deeply eroded?

One crucial step in rekindling intimacy is learning to make room for each other again—both physically and emotionally. When betrayal has torn you apart, it's natural to put up walls, retreat into your separate corners, and nurse your wounds alone. But true healing requires a willingness to come back together and create space in your hearts and your lives for the person you once cherished most.

Consider the story of Rachel and Adam. In the early months after Adam's affair came to light, Rachel could barely stand to be in the same room with him. The sight of his face, the sound of his voice, was enough to send her spiraling into rage and despair. She took to sleeping in the guest room, leaving for work early, and coming home late to avoid any chance of interaction.

For his part, Adam was drowning in shame and guilt. He knew he had shattered Rachel's trust and couldn't blame her for wanting nothing to do with him. So he retreated into his world of self-loathing and isolation, convinced that he deserved every ounce of misery he felt.

But as the weeks turned into months, Rachel and Adam began to realize that this separation was only compounding their pain. They missed the little moments of connection they used to share—the inside jokes, the lazy Sunday mornings, the comfort of falling asleep in each other's arms. Tentatively, they started to carve out small pockets of time together—a quick lunch here, a shared TV show there. It wasn't much, but it was a start.

Slowly but surely, Rachel and Adam began to make room for each other again. They started going to couples therapy, where they learned ways of making room in their lives for each other. The therapist suggested they find a way of putting out a welcome mat for each other. They set aside dedicated time each week to check in with each other without distractions or interruptions. They even started a new hobby together - hiking on the weekends - as a way to create shared experiences and memories.

It wasn't easy, and there were many setbacks and bumps along the way. But by consciously choosing to make space for each other - to prioritize their relationship even during great pain - Rachel and Adam slowly started to rebuild the intimacy they had lost. No one wants to be where they are not welcome. Making room for each other made them feel wanted and welcome again.

Making room for each other in the aftermath of an affair requires both physical and emotional effort. Practically, it means carving out dedicated time to be together—whether that's a nightly check-in, a weekly date night, or a monthly weekend away. It means putting down your phones, turning off the TV, and giving each other your full, undivided attention.

But it also means creating emotional space for your partner. It means setting aside your ego and defenses long enough to listen and empathize with their experience. It means being willing to be vulnerable and to share your thoughts, fears, and hopes, even when it feels scary or uncomfortable.

This can be especially challenging when trust has been broken, and emotions are running high. It's easy to fall into patterns of defensiveness, stonewalling, or contempt - all of which can quickly erode any sense of intimacy or connection.

That's why it's so important to approach this process with intention and care. Start small, with brief moments of quality time and simple gestures of affection and welcome. As you start to feel safer and more connected, gradually work up to deeper conversations and more vulnerable sharing.

Another helpful strategy is to focus on creating shared experiences and memories. Like Rachel and Adam's hiking trips, finding new hobbies or activities to enjoy together can help shift the focus from past pain to present connection. It gives you something positive to talk about and bond over and helps create a new chapter in your relationship story.

Of course, rebuilding intimacy after an affair is never a straight line. There will be days when you feel closer than ever and others when the gulf between you feels unbridgeable. The key is to keep showing up and making room, even when it feels hard or uncomfortable. This includes inviting them into your life and sharing events with them.

Take the example of Sophie and Liam. Even after months of therapy and intentional reconnection, Sophie still struggled with flashbacks and triggers around Liam's affair. Some days, the simplest glimpse of the other woman's name or the restaurant where they used to meet was enough to send her into a tailspin of anxiety and doubt.

In those moments, it was tempting for Sophie to shut down, to push Liam away and retreat into her pain. However, with practice and support, she learned to voice her struggles and allow Liam to comfort and reassure her. In turn, Liam learned to give Sophie the space she needed to process her emotions while making it clear that he was there for her whenever she was ready.

By continuing to make room for each other—even during great challenges and triggering—Sophie and Liam could weather the storms of recovery together. They learned that intimacy isn't about perfect harmony or perpetual bliss but rather the willingness to keep turning towards each other, day after day, season after season.

As you work to make room for each other in your relationship, remember to be patient and compassionate with yourselves. Rebuilding intimacy after betrayal is a brave and worthwhile pursuit, but it's also a deeply challenging one. Honor the fact that you're both wrestling with immense pain and uncertainty and that there will be times when connection feels impossible.

But also trust in the power of small, consistent efforts. Every moment of quality time, every vulnerable conversation, every shared laugh or tear - these are the building blocks of a new and deeper intimacy. By continuing to make room for each other, you create the conditions for genuine healing, resilience, and love to take root and grow.

Reflection Questions:

1. What small, practical ways can my partner and I make more room for each other in our daily lives and routines? How can I put out a welcome mat for them?

2. How can I practice setting aside my defenses and distractions to be more emotionally present and available to my partner?

3. What shared activities or experiences could we explore to help create new positive memories and a sense of connection in our relationship?

Chapter Nine

Threats to Avoid

"Those that are the loudest in their threats are the weakest in their actions." Charles Caleb Colton

As you and your partner work to rebuild intimacy after the affair, it's crucial to be aware of the potential threats that can derail your progress. These threats are often subtle, sneaking into your interactions and slowly eroding the trust and connection you've worked so hard to restore. But by learning to recognize and avoid them, you can create a stronger, more resilient foundation for your relationship.

One of the most common threats to intimacy after an affair is the use of absolutes and generalizations in your communication. When emotions run high, and wounds are still raw, it's easy to slip into language like "you always" or "you never." But these sweeping statements rarely reflect the full truth of your relationship, and they can quickly put your partner on the defensive.

Take the example of Megan and Chris. As they navigated the rocky road of affair recovery, Megan found herself constantly on guard, waiting for any sign that Chris might betray her again. In her hypervigilance, she would often lash out with accusations like, "You're always so secretive with your phone" or "You never tell me where you're going anymore."

While Megan's fears were understandable, given the deep betrayal she had experienced, her use of absolutes only served to push Chris further away. He felt like he could never win; no matter how hard he tried to be transparent and reliable, She could not be persuaded by facts or changes in his behavior. Megan would always find fault and make her statements.

It wasn't until their couples therapist pointed out Megan's language's damaging impact that she shifted her approach. Instead of relying on generalizations, she learned to express her concerns in more specific, situational terms. "When you took that phone call in the other room last night, I felt anxious and worried. Can we talk about what was going on there?" By focusing on concrete examples and her own emotional experience, Megan was able to invite Chris into a more productive dialogue and avoid putting him on the defensive.

Another threat to intimacy after infidelity is the tendency to make assumptions about your partner's thoughts, feelings, or intentions. Without clear communication, it's all too easy to fill in the blanks with our worst fears and insecurities. But when we act on these assumptions as if they're facts, we risk creating a self-fulfilling prophecy of disconnection and mistrust.

This was the case for Lauren and Mike. As they worked to rebuild their marriage after Mike's affair, Lauren found herself constantly second-guessing his every move. If he came home late from work, she assumed he must be cheating again. If he was quieter than usual, she took it as a sign that he was pulling away from her.

In reality, Mike was often struggling with his own guilt and shame around the affair, and his withdrawn behavior was more about his internal turmoil than any lack of love or commitment to Lauren. However, Lauren never asked him about his experience, so her assumptions only drove them further apart and sent her into a dark place.

They could start rebuilding authentic intimacy when Lauren learned to check her assumptions and approach Mike with curiosity and openness. Instead of accusing him of infidelity every time he was late, she said, "I noticed you've been working later than usual this week. How are you feeling about your job and workload right now?" By giving Mike space to share his perspective, Lauren was often able to defuse her own worst fears and foster a deeper sense of understanding between them.

A third threat to intimacy in the aftermath of an affair is the use of score-keeping and tit-for-tat thinking. When trust has been shattered, it's understandable to want to even the scales and make your partner feel the depth of your pain. However, engaging in revenge affairs or constantly pointing out your partner's mistakes will only breed more resentment and dysfunction in your relationship.

This was something that David and Erica struggled with intensely in the months following Erica's infidelity. For David, the urge to lash out, to punish Erica for the way she had hurt him, was almost irresistible. He would bring up her affair in every argument, using it as a trump card to shut down any complaint or critique she had about his behavior. He knew it made her feel bad about herself and would shut her down anytime things were unpleasant.

On some level, David knew that his score-keeping was only making things worse. But in his mind, it felt like the only way to regain some sense of power and control in a situation that had left him feeling so helpless and emasculated. It was only through a lot of individual therapy and self-reflection that David was able to let go of his need for revenge and start focusing on his healing and growth.

As you work to rebuild intimacy with your partner, try to be mindful of any urges towards score-keeping or revenge. Remind yourself that healing is not a competition and that causing your partner more pain will not alleviate your own. Instead, focus on expressing your needs and boundaries clearly and directly without using the affair as a weapon or bargaining chip.

Of course, avoiding these threats to intimacy is often easier said than done. When you're in the thick of affair recovery, it can feel like every interaction is fraught with potential landmines and triggers. That's why it's so important to approach this process with compassion - both for your partner and yourself.

Remember that you're both human and that rebuilding trust and intimacy after betrayal is messy. There will be moments of connection and moments of setback, times when you feel closer than ever, and times when the gulf between you feels unbridgeable. The key is to keep showing up and to keep choosing each other and your relationship, even when it feels hard or scary.

One helpful way to do this is to create a shared vision or intention for your relationship moving forward. What kind of partnership do you want to build together? What values and principles do you want to prioritize? Having a clear sense of your shared goals and commitments allows you to orient yourselves toward growth and healing, even amidst the inevitable challenges and setbacks.

Another key is to prioritize self-care and self-reflection throughout this process. As much as affair recovery is about repairing your relationship, it's also about tending to your own emotional and psychological wounds. Make sure you're carving out time for activities that nourish and replenish you, whether that's therapy, journaling, exercise, or creative pursuits. The more grounded and centered you are in yourself, the better equipped you'll be to show up fully and authentically in your relationship.

Self-care also includes having a healthy diet. Nutrition is important in maintaining healthy thinking and moods. This also includes not overeating or overindulging. Taking good care of yourself is another way of showing your spouse you care about them.

Ultimately, rebuilding intimacy after an affair is a courageous act of faith and resilience. It requires a willingness to be vulnerable and risk being hurt again for a deeper, more honest connection. It demands patience, humility, and a profound commitment to growth - both individually and as a couple.

But when you're able to navigate these challenges together, when you're able to face your deepest fears and insecurities and choose love anyway, that's when true healing and transformation become possible. That's when you can start to build an intimacy that's not just repaired but truly forged in the fire of your shared struggle and resilience.

Reflection Questions:

1. What patterns or habits in my communication might unintentionally threaten our intimacy (e.g., absolutes, assumptions, scorekeeping)? How can I gently redirect myself in those moments?

2. What is my greatest fear or insecurity regarding rebuilding intimacy with my partner? How might I express this vulnerability in a way that invites connection and understanding?

3. What is one small, concrete step I can take this week to prioritize my own self-care and emotional well-being amidst the challenges of affair recovery?

4. What fears or resentments are keeping me from getting closer to my spouse?

Chapter Ten

Sharing Your Emotions

"The value of emotions comes from sharing them, not simply having them."-Simon Senek

In the aftermath of an affair, emotions can feel like a minefield. The intensity of betrayal, hurt, anger, and fear can be overwhelming, leaving both partners raw and reeling. It's easy to want to shut down, to numb out, or to lash out in an attempt to protect your battered heart.

But as counterintuitive as it may feel, one of the most crucial steps in rebuilding intimacy after infidelity is learning to share your emotions with each other in a healthy, productive way. When you're able to express your deepest feelings – and to receive your partner's in turn – you create a bridge of understanding and empathy that can help you weather even the toughest storms together.

Of course, this is easier said than done. Many of us have learned to suppress or minimize our emotions, to put on a brave face and soldier on, even when we're crumbling inside. We may have grown up in families where vulnerability was seen as weakness or certain emotions (like anger or sadness) were discouraged or punished. Some may even be so out of touch with their emotions that they don't even have a label for what they are feeling.

This was the case for Sarah and Jake. Growing up, Sarah had always been the "strong one" in her family – the one who cared for everyone else's needs and never complained about her own. When Jake's affair shattered their marriage, Sarah found herself struggling to express the depth of her pain and betrayal. Whenever she tried to talk to Jake about how she was feeling, she would quickly get choked up and change the subject, insisting she was "fine" even as the tears threatened to spill over. She knew she felt something but didn't even have a word for it.

Jake, for his part, had his struggles with emotional expression. As a man, he had always been taught to keep a tight lid on his feelings and to never show weakness or vulnerability. In the aftermath of his affair, he was drowning in shame and regret, but he had no idea how to put those feelings into words. Whenever Sarah tried to get him to open up, he would shut down or get defensive, leaving them both feeling even more alone and disconnected.

It wasn't until Sarah and Jake started working with a couples therapist that they learned the tools for healthy emotional expression. Their therapist taught them about the four main categories of emotions—mad, sad, glad, and afraid—and encouraged them to start identifying and naming their feelings in real-time. Although they asked for hints, the therapist allowed them to struggle with identifying what they were feeling.

At first, it felt awkward and uncomfortable. Sarah worried that if she really let herself feel the depth of her pain, she would shatter into a million pieces. Jake feared that if he admitted to his shame and regret, Sarah would never be able to forgive him. But with practice and patience, they slowly started to crack open and let each other in.

One turning point came when Sarah finally allowed herself to break down in front of Jake. They were in the middle of a heated argument about his ongoing contact with the other woman, and Sarah could feel the familiar tightness in her throat, the pressure building behind her eyes. But instead of swallowing it back like she usually did, she let the tears come.

"I'm just so scared," she sobbed, her voice cracking. "I'm scared that you'll leave me again, that I'll never be enough for you. I'm scared that I'll never be able to trust you again, that this pain will never go away."

For Jake, seeing Sarah's raw vulnerability was a wake-up call. He realized how much she had been holding back, how much she had been suffering in silence. He felt a rush of empathy and love for her, and for the first time since the affair, he allowed himself to feel the weight of what he had done.

"I'm so sorry," he said, his own eyes filling with tears. "I'm sorry for hurting you, for betraying your trust, and for making you feel like you weren't enough. You are more than enough, Sarah. You're everything to me."

In that moment of shared vulnerability, Sarah and Jake felt a glimmer of the connection they had lost. They created a moment of profound intimacy and understanding by allowing themselves to fully feel and express their emotions.

Of course, learning to share your emotions in a healthy way is a process. Neither of them grew up in the healthiest of families; this was a whole new way of doing things. It requires ongoing practice, patience, and commitment from both partners. Here are a few key strategies to keep in mind:

1. Name your feelings.

When you're experiencing a strong emotion, it can be hard to think clearly or articulate what's going on inside. By simply naming the feeling—"I'm feeling really angry right now" or "I'm feeling so sad and alone"—you can create a bit of space and clarity for yourself. It also helps your partner understand and empathize with your experience.

2. Use "I" statements.

When expressing your emotions, try to focus on your own experience rather than blaming or attacking your partner. Instead of saying, "You make me so mad when you do that," try, "I feel really angry and frustrated when X happens." This helps keep the conversation focused on understanding and connection rather than criticism and defensiveness.

3. Be specific.

The more specific you can be about what you're feeling and why, the more your partner will be able to understand and respond to your needs. Instead of just saying, "I'm upset," try, "I'm feeling hurt and betrayed right now because of X."

4. Allow space for your partner's emotions.

Just as you need to express your feelings, it is important to create space for your partner to do the same. This means listening when they share, resisting the urge to jump in with fixes or defensiveness, and validating their experience even if you see things differently. Part of allowing space includes giving them time and silence to experience their emotions. When you rush in to fill the silence, you are also interrupting their ability to get in touch with their emotions.

5. Practice self-compassion.

Sharing your emotions – especially the messy, vulnerable ones – can be scary and uncomfortable. Be gentle with yourself as you learn this new skill, and remember that it's okay to take breaks or set boundaries when you need to.

One couple that exemplifies the power of emotional sharing is Alex and Maggie. In the early days of their affair recovery, they struggled to have a conversation that didn't devolve into yelling, blaming, and icy silences. But with the help of their therapist, they slowly learned to tune into their emotions and express them in a way that brought them closer together.

Maggie realized that beneath her simmering anger was a deep well of sadness and fear—sadness for the dreams and trust that had been shattered and fear that she would never feel safe or loved again. She recognized she worried about the future rather than focusing attention on the present. When she shared these more vulnerable feelings with Alex, he responded with empathy and reassurance rather than the defensiveness that her anger often triggered.

Similarly, Alex learned to confront the shame and self-loathing that drove many of his avoidant and minimizing behaviors. When he told Maggie, "I feel so disgusted with myself for what I did, and I'm terrified that you'll never be able to look at me the same way again," she offered him the forgiveness and acceptance he craved.

By sharing their deepest emotions – the good, the bad, and the ugly – Alex and Maggie slowly rebuilt the intimacy and trust that had been lost. Initially, they found expressing emotions easier than hearing each other without reacting. They learned that they could handle each other's pain and fear, that they could sit with each other in the darkest moments and still choose love and commitment.

Sharing your emotions after an affair is a courageous act of vulnerability and trust. It requires peeling back the layers of self-protection and inviting your partner into your heart's raw, tender places. It means learning to sit with discomfort, to tolerate messy and conflicting feelings, and to offer each other grace and compassion along the way.

But when you can do this hard work together – to see and be seen by each other – you open the door to a deeper, more authentic intimacy than you ever thought possible. You build the kind of bond that can weather any storm, a love that is tested by fire and comes out stronger on the other side.

Reflection Questions:

1. What emotions do I struggle to express, and why? How might I practice getting more comfortable with sharing these feelings?

2. How can I create a safe, non-judgmental space for my partner to express their emotions, even when those emotions are difficult for me to hear?

3. What is one specific way I can practice self-compassion and gentleness with myself as I learn to be more emotionally vulnerable in my relationship?

4. How were emotions handled in my family of origin? What patterns or habits about emotions am I doing?

Chapter Eleven

Regaining Objectivity

"Dispassionate objectivity is itself a passion, for the real and for the truth."
Abraham Maslow

Everything you thought you knew about your partner, your relationship, and even yourself have been called into question after an affair. Amid such emotional turmoil, it's easy to lose sight of objectivity - to get swept up in a spiral of fear, anger, and despair that colors your every interaction and decision. It happened to you, and it's hard not to take it personally. In taking it personally, you lose your objectivity.

But as hard as it may be, regaining a sense of objectivity is crucial for healing and moving forward after infidelity. When you can step back from the intensity of your emotions and view your situation with a more balanced, clear-eyed perspective, you open the door to new possibilities and solutions that may have been obscured by pain and reactivity.

One couple that struggled with this in the early stages of their recovery was Liam and Emily. When Emily first discovered Liam's affair, she was understandably devastated. She couldn't eat, sleep, or focus on anything other than the searing pain of betrayal. In her mind, Liam had transformed from the loving, devoted husband she thought she knew into a cruel, selfish stranger who deliberately shattered her world.

Liam, meanwhile, was drowning in his guilt and shame. He knew he had made a terrible mistake and desperately wanted to make things right with Emily. But whenever he tried to apologize or express remorse, Emily would lash out with biting accusations and contempt. In her eyes, nothing he could say or do would ever be enough to make up for what he had done. He saw little to no love in her eyes for him.

Liam and Emily remained stuck in this destructive cycle as the weeks turned into months. Emily was so consumed by her pain and anger that she couldn't see any of Liam's efforts to change or make amends. Liam, in turn, began to feel hopeless and resentful, wondering if he could ever earn back Emily's trust and forgiveness. He wondered if it was worth it.

It wasn't until they started working with a skilled therapist that Liam and Emily regained some objectivity in their situation. Their therapist helped them see how their intense emotions were keeping them trapped in a cycle of blame and defensiveness, preventing them from really hearing or understanding each other.

With practice and guidance, Emily learned to take a step back when she felt herself getting triggered or reactive. Instead of immediately lashing out at Liam, she would take a few deep breaths and ask herself, "What am I feeling right now? What do I need in this moment?" This helped her get in touch with the deeper fears and insecurities beneath her anger and communicate them to Liam so that he could understand and respond to them. Instead of attacking Liam anytime she was upset, she learned instead to let him know what she needed at those moments.

Liam, meanwhile, learned to be more patient and understanding with Emily's outbursts. Instead of getting defensive or shutting down, he practiced listening to her pain and acknowledging the impact of his actions. He also worked on taking responsibility for his healing and growth rather than relying on Emily to "get over it" or forgive him on his timeline.

As they both practiced stepping back and looking at their situation more objectively, Liam and Emily began to see glimmers of hope and possibility that had been obscured by their pain. They realized that as devastating as the affair had been, it was also an opportunity to really examine the weaknesses and disconnects in their relationship and work together to build something stronger and more authentic.

As with most all of recovery, regaining objectivity after an affair is easier said than done. When you're in the thick of such intense emotional pain, it can feel impossible to see your situation clearly or make rational decisions. But with time, practice, and support, it is possible to start shifting your perspective and finding your way back to solid ground. They had to get out of a reactive way of thinking and into a problem-solving way of thinking.

One key strategy is to focus on the present and the future rather than getting lost in the past. It's natural to want to obsess over the details of the affair, replay every moment, and analyze every interaction for clues about what went wrong. But at a certain point, this becomes more harmful than helpful—it keeps you stuck in a loop of pain and resentment rather than allowing you to move forward. It keeps the pain churning in your mind rather than moving forward.

Instead, try to bring your attention to the here and now. What is the current state of your relationship? What steps can you take today to start rebuilding trust and connection? What kind of future do you want to create together, and what changes must happen to make that possible?

Another helpful practice is to cultivate compassion - both for yourself and for your partner. When you're feeling triggered or reactive, remind yourself that you're both human beings struggling to navigate an incredibly difficult situation. Your partner is not a monster; you are not a fool for loving them. You're both flawed, complex individuals doing your best to heal and grow.

This doesn't mean excusing or minimizing the impact of the affair. It is important to hold your partner accountable for their actions and set clear boundaries around what you need to feel safe and respected moving forward. But approaching the process with compassion can help you stay grounded and maintain perspective, even in the face of intense emotions.

Gabriel and Olivia, another couple navigating the aftermath of infidelity, found that practicing compassion was key to regaining their objectivity. When Olivia first found out about Gabriel's affair, she was filled with a white-hot rage. She couldn't imagine ever being able to forgive him, let alone rebuild their relationship.

However, as she worked with her therapist, Olivia began to explore the deeper roots of her anger. She realized that beneath her fury was a profound sense of fear and inadequacy—a belief that she wasn't enough and that she would never be able to truly satisfy or keep Gabriel's love. Her anger was about herself and Gabriel as well. Anytime she felt inadequate, her solution was to react with anger.

As she shared these vulnerable feelings with Gabriel, he responded with empathy and reassurance. He acknowledged how his behavior had triggered and reinforced Olivia's insecurities and committed to being more transparent and attuned to her needs moving forward.

In turn, Olivia practiced extending compassion to Gabriel. She recognized that his infidelity was not about her inadequacy but about his unhealed wounds and poor coping mechanisms. She didn't excuse his actions but could see them in a more nuanced, human light. Part of him feared her, leading him to hide things from her.

By approaching each other with compassion and understanding, Gabriel and Olivia could start dismantling the walls of blame and defensiveness that had kept them stuck. They could see their situation more objectively, not as an irrevocable shattering, but as a painful yet transformative opportunity for growth.

Regaining objectivity after an affair is an ongoing process. There will be moments when you slip back into old patterns of reactivity and blame when your pain feels so overwhelming that you can't see a way forward. In those moments, be gentle with yourself. Remind yourself that setbacks are a normal part of the process.

But also trust that by being committed to each other, practicing better techniques for connecting, and having time, you can start to see your situation with clearer eyes. You can learn to step back from the intensity of your emotions and make choices based on your deepest values and aspirations. You can find your way back to yourself, your partner, and the love you once shared - not by erasing the past but by weaving it into a new, more honest, and resilient chapter of your story.

Reflection Questions:

1. What emotions or reactions tend to pull me out of objectivity and into a more reactive, distorted view of my situation? How can I practice noticing and gently shifting these patterns?

2. In what ways might practicing compassion - for myself, my partner, and our relationship - help me maintain perspective and clarity as we navigate healing?

3. What is one small step I can take today to build a more balanced, objective view of my relationship and our potential for growth and repair?

Taking Action

Part Four

Restore The Family Press

Chapter Twelve

Consistency and Time

"It's about consistency." Ryan Tannehill

When it comes to affair recovery, there are no quick fixes or magic solutions. Healing from the trauma of betrayal and rebuilding a relationship shattered by infidelity is a journey that requires many things. One of those is consistency over time.

It's easy to get caught up in the idea that there should be some grand, sweeping gesture or breakthrough moment that will suddenly make everything better. We want to believe that if we just find the right words, the perfect apology, or the ultimate act of contrition, we can put the pain of the affair behind us and move on as if it never happened. With one magic zap, all will be remedied.

But the truth is, affair recovery is less about those big, dramatic moments and more about the small, daily choices and actions that slowly but surely create a new foundation for trust, intimacy, and connection to grow. It's about showing up, day after day, even when you're tired, scared, or triggered. It's about choosing to have difficult conversations, extending empathy and understanding, and taking responsibility for your healing and growth.

Take the story of Valerie and Chris. When Valerie discovered Chris's affair with a coworker, she was understandably devastated. She couldn't imagine how they could ever move past such a profound betrayal, and for a long time, it seemed like they wouldn't. They would have explosive arguments followed by icy silences and tearful apologies followed by bitter recriminations. The good moments were fleeting and far between.

But slowly, with the help of couples therapy and a lot of hard work, Valerie and Chris began to find their way back to each other. They learned to communicate more honestly and effectively and to express their feelings without attacking or shutting down. They created new rituals of connection, like daily check-ins and weekly date nights, to prioritize their relationship and rebuild intimacy.

It wasn't straightforward by any means. There were plenty of setbacks and moments of doubt along the way. However, by staying consistent in their efforts and standing up for each other even when it was hard, Valerie and Chris gradually started to heal the wounds of the past and create a new, stronger bond.

Maintaining open, honest communication is key to consistency in affair recovery. This means regular check-ins with your partner, even when you don't like it. It means being willing to express your thoughts and feelings, even when they're messy or uncomfortable. It also means listening to your partner's experience without judgment or defensiveness.

This can be especially challenging in the early stages of recovery when emotions are raw and triggers are frequent. It's natural to want to avoid difficult conversations or sweep things under the rug to keep the peace. But avoiding the hard stuff only allows resentment and disconnection to fester.

Instead, try to approach communication with a spirit of curiosity and vulnerability. Set aside regular times to discuss how you're both doing and what's working and not in your recovery process. There are no "one size fits all" relationship solutions. Be honest about your fears, needs, and hopes for the future. And when your partner is sharing their own experience, really try to put yourself in their shoes and understand where they're coming from.

Another important aspect of consistency is following through on your commitments and actions. If you've promised to be more transparent about your whereabouts or to cut off contact with the affair partner, you must stick to those agreements, even when it's inconvenient or challenging.

This is something that Derek and Sophia struggled with in the aftermath of Derek's affair. In the early days of their recovery, Derek swore up and down that he would do whatever it took to earn back Sophia's trust. He agreed to share his phone and email passwords, always let her know where he was going and with whom he was, and go to individual therapy to work on his issues.

However, as time passed, the immediate crisis faded, and Derek started slipping back into old patterns. He would "forget" to tell Sophia about a work happy hour or delete a text message from a female friend because he "didn't want her to worry." To Sophia, these small lapses felt like massive betrayals, proof that Derek wasn't serious about changing.

It took Derek many tough conversations and recommitment to start rebuilding that trust. He realized that consistency wasn't just about the big, showy gestures but about the small, daily acts of integrity and fol-low-through. He learned to prioritize transparency and honesty, even when uncomfortable because he knew that was the only way to truly heal their relationship.

Consistency is also about making room for both partners' healing processes, even when they don't perfectly align. After an affair, it's common for the betrayed partner to have intense fluctuations in their emotions and readiness to move forward. One day they may feel hopeful and forgiving, the next they may be consumed by rage and despair.

As the partner who had the affair, it can be tempting to put pressure on them to "get over it" or reach some arbitrary milestone of forgiveness. But true healing can't be rushed or forced. It's important to allow your partner the time and space they need to work through their feelings, even if the process is messy or nonlinear.

At the same time, the partner who had the affair must also commit to their consistent growth and change. It's not enough to wait for forgiveness or expect your partner to do all the heavy lifting of rebuilding trust. You must be proactive in examining your patterns, attending to your healing, and showing through your actions that you are dedicated to being a safer, more trustworthy partner.

For Naomi and Jose, finding this balance of consistency and patience was key to their recovery. Naomi, who had been betrayed, had days where she felt consumed by obsessive thoughts and triggers related to the affair. She would lash out at Jose with accusations and contempt, convinced he would never truly change.

Jose, for his part, struggled not to take Naomi's outbursts personally or get defensive. He had to learn to give her space to express her pain, even when it was hard to hear, while still maintaining his boundaries and commitment to growth. He consistently attended therapy, shared his feelings and progress with Naomi, and found ways to show her through his daily actions that he was dedicated to being a better man.

Over time, as they both stayed consistent in their efforts, Naomi and Jose began to find a new rhythm in their relationship. The bad days became less frequent and intense, the good days longer and more joyful. They developed a deeper understanding and appreciation for each other's struggles and strengths. Slowly but surely, they started to build a partnership that felt more authentic, intimate, and resilient than ever before.

If you're in the thick of affair recovery right now, the idea of consistency and patience may feel daunting or even impossible. When you're riding the roller coaster of intense emotions and trust violations, it's hard to imagine ever finding your way to stable ground.

But know that healing is possible, one small, consistent step at a time. By committing to consistent efforts, following through on your promises, allowing room for both partners' processes, and staying dedicated to your growth, you can slowly but surely create a new foundation of love and trust.

It won't be a perfect journey. There will be moments of fear, frustration, and doubt. But by showing up for yourself and each other, day after day, you open the door to genuine transformation. You build the kind of love tested by fire and come out stronger, wiser, and more beautiful on the other side.

Reflection Questions:

1. What small, daily actions can I commit to to build consistency and trust in my relationship?

2. How can I practice patience and understanding for my partner's healing process, even when it feels difficult or triggering?

3. What do I need to feel safe and supported as I consistently work on my growth and change? How can I communicate those needs to my partner?

Chapter Thirteen

Know Where You Stand

"Going for character: why not now, and where you stand?" Robert Louis Stevenson

Imagine you're on a long, arduous hike through unfamiliar terrain. The path ahead is steep and winding, the landscape dotted with obstacles and pitfalls, ascents and descents. Now imagine navigating this journey without a map or compass, without any sense of where you are or where you're headed. Sounds daunting, right?

In many ways, affair recovery can feel like this kind of disorienting, uphill battle. When you're in the thick of healing from betrayal, it's easy to feel lost, confused, and unsure of your footing. The familiar landmarks of your relationship have been upended, and the future you once envisioned may now seem hazy and uncertain.

That's why one of the most critical steps in the recovery process is gaining clarity about where you stand - both as individuals and as a couple. It's about taking stock of your current reality, assessing your progress and setbacks, and charting a course forward based on your unique needs, values, and goals.

Consider the story of Lauren and David. When David's affair first came to light, Lauren felt like her entire world had been turned upside down.

She couldn't eat, sleep, or focus on anything other than the searing pain of betrayal. She oscillated between intense bouts of anger and debilitating sadness, unsure how she would ever be able to trust David again.

David, for his part, was drowning in shame and remorse. He knew he had made a terrible mistake and was willing to do anything to make things right. But he struggled to know how to support Lauren in her healing while also tending to his own conflicted emotions and unmet needs.

For months, they stumbled forward in a haze of pain and confusion, their interactions largely defined by Lauren's triggers and David's defensiveness. They would have fleeting moments of connection and hope, only to be followed by explosive arguments that left them both feeling hopeless and drained.

It wasn't until they started working with a skilled couples therapist that Lauren and David began to gain some clarity on their situation. With guidance and support, they learned to step back from the daily ups and downs of recovery and take a more honest, objective look at their situation.

They asked themselves tough questions like: What progress have we made so far, and what areas still need work? What are our individual and shared goals for healing, and are we both fully committed to the process? What old patterns or unmet needs contributed to the affair, and how can we address them moving forward?

By gaining this kind of clarity and perspective, Lauren and David were able to start making more informed, intentional choices about their recovery. They began gaining a feel for where their relationship was. They identified specific areas where they needed to focus their efforts, like improving communication and rebuilding trust. They set realistic milestones for their healing journey and celebrated each small victory along the way.

Of course, gaining clarity in affair recovery is rarely straightforward or one-time. As you move through the ups and downs of healing, your sense of where you stand may shift and evolve. What feels like progress one day may feel like a setback the next. What seems like a shared goal at one point may later reveal itself to be more one-sided.

That's why it's so important to keep checking in with yourself and your partner throughout the recovery process. Set aside regular times to reflect on your journey so far and recalibrate your path forward as needed. This might look like weekly check-ins where you share your thoughts, feelings, and concerns or monthly "state of the union" conversations where you assess your overall progress and set intentions for the coming weeks.

It can also be helpful to seek outside support to gain clarity, whether that's through individual or couples therapy, coaching, or support groups. Sometimes, an objective third party can help you see your situation with fresh eyes and offer valuable insights and tools for navigating the path ahead.

Another key aspect of knowing where you stand is being honest about your non-negotiables and deal-breakers. You need to feel safe, respected, and valued in your relationship - the bare minimum requirements for you to be able to stay and continue doing the work of recovery.

For Caitlyn, who had been betrayed by her husband Jacob's affair, one non-negotiable was complete transparency about his devices and where-abouts. She needed to know that she could check Jacob's phone or email at any time without fear of what she might find. She needed him to be upfront about his schedule and plans and to proactively communicate any changes or delays.

At first, Jacob bristled at these requirements, seeing them as a lack of trust and an invasion of his privacy. However, through honest conversations and their therapist's guidance, he understood that this level of transparency was necessary for Caitlyn to feel safe enough to rebuild trust.

It wasn't a punishment or a permanent state of affairs but a crucial stepping stone in their healing process.

Caitlyn created a stronger foundation for their recovery by being clear and firm in her non-negotiables. She knew that she was prioritizing her own healing and self-respect while also giving Jacob the opportunity to demonstrate his commitment through consistent, trustworthy actions. Over time, as they both showed up with integrity and worked to address the root issues behind the affair, the need for such stringent transparency naturally lessened.

Of course, non-negotiables can look different for every couple and every individual. For some, it might be the need for a sincere apology or a commitment to individual therapy. For others, it might be the willingness to totally and completely cut off contact with the affair partner or make significant changes to prioritize the relationship.

What's important is that you clarify what you need to feel safe and respected in your relationship and communicate those needs clearly and assertively. This isn't about making ultimatums or trying to control your partner but about honoring your boundaries and giving your relationship the best possible chance at healing.

Remember that knowing where you stand is an ongoing, evolving process as you continue your recovery journey. Keep checking in with yourself and your partner, assessing your progress and setbacks, and adjusting your course as needed. Above all, keep anchoring yourself in your truth and integrity—the unshakeable knowledge of what you need, value, and work towards.

By staying committed to clarity and self-honesty, you give yourself the greatest gift of all: the ability to navigate even the rockiest terrain with courage, compassion, and an unwavering sense of direction. You may not have a perfect map for the journey ahead, but you'll have something even better - a deep, abiding trust in your resilience and the potential for growth and healing within you and your relationship.

Reflection Questions:

1. What are my non-negotiables for feeling safe and respected in my relationship as we navigate affair recovery?

2. How can I continue to gain clarity on my own needs, values, and goals throughout the healing process? What practices or support systems can help me stay anchored in self-honesty?

3. What kind of regular check-ins or conversations can my partner and I have to assess our progress, recalibrate our path forward, and ensure we're on the same page in our recovery?

4. What are my deal breakers, and how will I deal with them?

Chapter Fourteen

When to Seek Help

"One of the biggest defects in life is the inability to ask for help." Robert Kiyosaki

Affair recovery is a deeply personal and challenging journey that requires significant emotional labor, commitment to change, and resilience. While couples can navigate this process on their own, there are times when seeking outside help is not only beneficial but truly necessary for healing and growth.

It's a bit like setting out on a long, complex hiking trail. You might have a map and a compass, a backpack full of supplies, and a determined spirit. But there may come a point where the terrain gets too steep, the path too obscured, and the obstacles too overwhelming to tackle alone. In those moments, having a skilled guide - someone who knows the landscape and can offer expert support and direction - can make all the difference.

The same is true for affair recovery. While this book provides a roadmap and tools for the journey, there may be times when you need a professional's additional support and guidance to keep moving forward.

So, how do you know when it's time to bring in outside support? Here are a few key indicators:

1. You're stuck in a cycle of pain and reactivity.

If you find yourself having the same fights, triggering the same wounds, and falling into the same negative patterns over and over again, it may be a sign that you need help breaking the cycle. A skilled therapist can offer new insights and tools for managing triggers, communicating effectively, changing patterns, and healing underlying wounds.

2. You're struggling to rebuild trust and intimacy.

Rebuilding trust and intimacy after an affair is a delicate, complex process that requires patience, vulnerability, and skill. If you're finding it difficult to make progress in this area, a couples counselor who specializes in affair recovery can provide guidance and support tailored to your unique situation.

3. You're dealing with intense, persistent emotions.

Betrayal trauma can unleash a tidal wave of intense, overwhelming emotions - rage, despair, anxiety, shame, and more. If you're struggling to manage these emotions on your own, or if they're significantly interfering with your daily life and functioning, individual therapy can be a vital resource for processing and healing.

4. You have a history of trauma or mental health challenges.

If you or your partner have a history of trauma, addiction, family history of affairs, or mental health issues, the impact of an affair can be even more destabilizing and complex. In these cases, working with a therapist who specializes in trauma recovery or dual diagnosis can be essential for addressing the full scope of your healing needs.

5. Your relationship was unhealthy or dysfunctional before the affair.

If your relationship was already marked by unhealthy patterns, poor communication, or unresolved conflicts before the affair, trying to heal and rebuild on your own may be particularly challenging. A couples therapist can help you identify and transform these underlying issues as you work towards recovery.

For Elena and Marcus, seeking professional help came after months of painful, circular arguments and failed attempts to rebuild trust. Elena, who had been betrayed, was struggling with intense anxiety and hyper-vigilance, constantly monitoring Marcus's every move for signs of further deception. Marcus, in turn, would vacillate between defensiveness and self-flagellation, unsure how to reassure Elena or make amends in a way that truly landed.

It was a chance conversation with a friend who had been through a similar situation that finally convinced them to take the leap. "I know it feels scary and vulnerable to bring someone else into your recovery process," their friend said, "but for us, it was truly the turning point. Our therapist helped us see our wounds and patterns with so much more clarity and compassion and gave us concrete tools for rebuilding our connection. I can't imagine where we'd be without that support."

With some trepidation, Elena and Marcus set out to find a couples counselor who specialized in affair recovery. They asked for recommendations from friends and read online reviews, ultimately choosing a therapist who felt like a good fit for their needs and values. And while the process was far from easy - there were plenty of tearful, uncomfortable moments in those early sessions - they slowly began to see glimmers of progress and hope.

Their therapist helped them establish new norms and boundaries around communication, teaching them how to express their feelings and needs without blame or defensiveness. She guided them through exercises to rebuild trust and intimacy, like taking turns planning special dates or sharing vulnerable parts of their stories. And she helped them explore the deeper roots of the affair, the unspoken fears, unmet needs, and unhealthy patterns that had left their relationship vulnerable in the first place.

Over time, with consistent effort and the steady support of their therapist, Elena and Marcus began to heal and reconnect in ways they never thought possible. They learned to see each other - and themselves - with greater compassion and understanding. They developed new rituals of connection, joy, and a shared vision for the marriage they wanted to build. And while the scar of the affair would always be a part of their story, it no longer defined them or held them back from the love and life they desired.

Of course, seeking professional help for affair recovery isn't always straightforward. There can be logistical barriers like cost, scheduling, location, and emotional obstacles like shame, fear, or resistance to change. It's important to acknowledge and work through these challenges as they arise rather than letting them deter you from the support you need.

If cost is a concern, consider looking for sliding-scale or low-cost therapy options in your community or exploring whether your insurance covers mental health services. If scheduling is a challenge, get creative and proactive - could you do early morning or lunchtime sessions or find a therapist who offers weekend appointments? If location is an issue, consider expanding your search to include online or teletherapy options, which have become increasingly common and effective in recent years.

And if you're dealing with emotional blocks around seeking help, try to approach them with curiosity and compassion. What fears or beliefs come up when you think about therapy? What past experiences or messages might be influencing your resistance? How might you reframe seeking help as an act of strength, commitment, and self-love?

Remember, too, that seeking professional support for affair recovery is not a one-size-fits-all process. Some couples may find that a few months of intensive therapy is enough to get them back on track, while others may benefit from ongoing support over a longer period. Some may thrive with traditional talk therapy, while others may find alternative modalities like EMDR, somatic experiencing, or art therapy to be particularly helpful.

The key is to stay open, curious, and committed to your healing journey and trust that the right resources and support will reveal themselves as you take each step forward. Know that no matter how alone or stuck you may feel in a given moment, there is always help and hope available—you need only reach out and ask.

As Travis and Olivia discovered in their recovery journey, sometimes the bravest and most transformative thing you can do is simply admit that you need support beyond yourselves. After months of trying to heal and rebuild on their own following Travis's affair, they finally reached a breaking point - the pain and distrust had become too much to bear, and they knew they couldn't keep going in the same cycles of conflict and disconnection.

It was Olivia who first suggested seeking couples therapy after a particularly raw and revelatory conversation one evening. "I love you, and I want to make this work," she said through tears, "but I don't think we can do it alone anymore. We need help - I need help - to find a way through this pain and back to each other. What do you think about finding a therapist who can guide us?"

Travis was initially resistant - he worried that bringing a stranger into their most vulnerable struggles would only make things worse. He still had some pride, and part of him believed they should be able to fix things on their own. But seeing the desperation and sincerity in Olivia's eyes, he realized that his resistance was rooted more in fear than wisdom. He took a deep breath, reached for her hand, and said, "Okay. Let's do it. Let's find someone who can help us heal and grow together."

That decision was the turning point in their recovery journey. With the guidance and support of a skilled therapist, Travis and Olivia slowly began to untangle the knots of betrayal, resentment, and fear that had bound them for so long. They learned to communicate with greater clarity and compassion, to set healthy boundaries and express their needs, and to reconnect with the love and commitment that had first brought them together.

It wasn't a quick or easy process by any means. There were times when the pain felt just as raw and overwhelming as at the beginning, when old triggers and wounds would resurface with a vengeance. But now, instead of getting lost in the darkness, they had a steady light to guide them through - the light of their own courage and determination and the wisdom and care of a therapist who believed in their potential for healing.

Slowly but surely, that light grew stronger and steadier, illuminating new paths and possibilities for their relationship. They began to see each other - and themselves - with fresh eyes, to appreciate how their struggles had formed them into stronger, wiser, more compassionate partners. They discovered new depths of resilience and grace within themselves and learned to extend that same understanding to each other.

As they looked back on their journey months later, Travis and Olivia marveled at how far they had come—rebuilding their marriage and becoming the kind of people and partners they had always wanted to be. While they knew that the work of growth and healing would continue long beyond the therapist's office, they also knew that they now had the tools, the insight, and the support they needed to face whatever challenges lay ahead.

In the end, that's what seeking help for affair recovery is all about. It's not about finding a quick fix or a magic bullet but about gaining the resources and guidance you need to become the hero of your healing journey. It's about having the courage to reach out and ask for support when you feel lost or stuck, trusting that there are always new possibilities and pathways waiting to be discovered.

So if you find yourself at a crossroads in your recovery process, wondering if you can make it through the wilderness of betrayal and back to the love and life you desire - remember Travis and Olivia, Elena and Marcus, and all the other brave couples who have walked this path before you. There is no shame in seeking the help and support you need to heal and grow.

Most of all, remember that even in your darkest and most painful moments, you have within you an unshakable strength, wisdom, and capacity for love. With the right tools, support, and mindset, you can transform even the deepest wounds into opportunities for profound growth and connection—one brave, compassionate, imperfect step at a time.

Reflection Questions:

1. What signs or indicators have you noticed that suggest it might be time to seek professional help for your affair recovery process?

2. What fears, doubts or logistical concerns arise when you think about reaching out for therapy or counseling? How might you work through these barriers with compassion and creativity?

3. If you have sought therapy or other professional support in the past, what was helpful or unhelpful about the experience? What qualities or approaches would you look for in a therapist or counselor to support you in this current healing journey?

Chapter Fifteen

Affair Recovery Plan

"A goal without a plan is just a wish." - Antoine de Saint-Exupéry

Navigating the complex and emotional terrain of affair recovery can feel a lot like setting out on a long, unpredictable journey without GPS, a clear map, or a destination. You don't know where you are headed or even how to get there. You know you need to keep moving forward, but the path ahead is obscured by pain, confusion, and uncertainty. It's easy to feel lost, overwhelmed, and unsure of your next steps.

That's where having a clear, comprehensive affair recovery plan comes in. Much like a roadmap for a physical journey, an affair recovery plan provides a framework and guide for the emotional and relational work ahead. It helps you clarify your goals, identify potential obstacles and resources, and break the larger process into manageable, actionable steps.

Consider the story of Jenna and Michael. When Michael's affair first came to light, they were both reeling from the shock and devastation. Jenna oscillated between extremes of rage and despair, unsure how she would ever be able to trust Michael again. Consumed with guilt and shame, Michael struggled to find the right words or actions to repair the damage he had caused.

For weeks, they stumbled forward in a reactive, haphazard way, their interactions largely driven by Jenna's unpredictable emotions and Michael's clumsy attempts at damage control. They would have intense, circular conversations that left them both feeling drained and hopeless, followed by periods of tense silence and avoidance. They knew they needed to do something different but did not know where to start.

It was their couples therapist who first suggested creating an affair recovery plan. She explained that having a clear, agreed-upon roadmap for their healing work would help them stay focused and aligned, even during intense emotional upheaval. Together, they could identify their shared goals, anticipate potential setbacks, and outline specific actions and rituals to support their progress.

At first, the idea of creating a plan felt daunting and abstract. How could they possibly map out a journey that felt so unpredictable and overwhelming? How can you map a journey to a place you've never been? However, with their therapist's guidance, Jenna and Michael began to break down the process into smaller, more manageable pieces.

They started by clarifying their individual and shared intentions for the recovery work ahead. What did they each need to feel safe, respected, and supported in the process? What did rebuilding trust and intimacy look like for them? What kind of relationship did they ultimately want to create together? They established a clear direction and purpose for their efforts by articulating these larger goals and visions.

Next, they identified potential obstacles and triggers that could arise along the way. Jenna acknowledged that certain dates, places, or situations might be particularly challenging for her, triggering painful memories or fears related to the affair. Michael recognized that his shame and defensiveness could sometimes interfere with his ability to show up with empathy and accountability. By naming these potential roadblocks upfront, they could develop strategies and supports to navigate them more skillfully.

A key component of Jenna and Michael's recovery plan was establishing clear boundaries and agreements around trust and transparency. They identified specific actions and behaviors that were important for rebuilding safety and security in their relationship, such as Michael sharing his phone and email passwords, checking in regularly about his whereabouts and plans, and cutting off contact with the affair partner. He even went so far as to send her pictures of where he was. They also agreed on consequences and check-in points to ensure these agreements were consistently honored.

In addition to these practical steps, Jenna and Michael's plan included rituals and practices to nurture their emotional and relational healing. They committed to regular check-in conversations where they could share their feelings, concerns, and progress without judgment or defensiveness. They established a weekly date night to focus on reconnecting and enjoying each other's company, free from affair-related discussions. They each agreed to pursue individual therapy and self-care practices to support their growth and well-being throughout the process.

Of course, even with a thorough and thoughtful plan in place, Jenna and Michael's recovery journey was far from predictable. There were times when unexpected triggers or conflicts would arise, throwing them off course and reigniting old wounds. One was when Michael went to his high school reunion, where he was tempted to reconnect with some old flames. There were moments of profound despair and doubt when the path ahead seemed too daunting to continue.

But having a clear plan to return to in those moments made all the difference. When they felt lost or stuck, they could look to their roadmap and recommit to the next small step forward. When they struggled to understand or support each other, they could revisit their shared goals and values as a touchstone. And when progress felt slow or unsteady, they could celebrate the milestones and rituals that marked their hard work and resilience along the way.

Over time, as they continued to work their plan with diligence and devotion, Jenna and Michael began to see real, tangible shifts in their relationship. The raw, searing pain of betrayal began to soften and transform, making space for new experiences of understanding, empathy, and forgiveness. The trust and intimacy that had been shattered slowly began to reform, stronger and more authentic than before. And the larger vision they had identified for their relationship - one of honesty, growth, and unconditional love - began to feel not just possible but inevitable.

As Jenna reflected on their journey months later, she realized that their recovery plan had been so much more than just a set of strategies or actions. It had been an anchor and a north star, a container for their commitment and a catalyst for their transformation. It had given them a way to hold both the immense pain and the profound potential of the healing process, to stay true to themselves and each other even in the darkest and most uncertain times.

If you're in the midst of your affair recovery journey, creating a clear plan of action can be an immensely powerful and stabilizing force. It can help you move from a place of reactive chaos to intentional, purposeful growth and give you a way to measure and celebrate your progress along the way. Here are some key elements to consider as you craft your affair recovery plan:

1. Clarify your intentions and goals

What does real, lasting healing look like for you and your relationship? What do you each need to feel safe, respected, and supported in the process? What kind of future do you ultimately want to create together?

Spend time reflecting on these larger questions, and use them to guide and anchor your more specific actions and strategies.

2. Identify potential obstacles and triggers

What internal or external factors might make the recovery process more challenging for you? Are there certain situations, dynamics, or patterns that tend to escalate conflict or shut down communication? By anticipating these potential roadblocks, you can develop proactive strategies and support systems to navigate them more skillfully.

3. Establish clear boundaries and agreements

What specific actions, behaviors, or rituals are important for rebuilding trust and safety in your relationship? How will you handle transparency, communication, and accountability moving forward? Be as specific and concrete as possible in your agreements, and make sure to revisit and adjust them as needed along the way.

4. Prioritize emotional and relational healing

In addition to practical steps and strategies, ensure your plan includes rituals and practices to nurture your emotional and relational well-being. This might include regular check-in conversations, dedicated quality time, individual therapy or support groups, or shared self-care activities. The more you can attend to the deeper layers of healing and connection, the more sustainable and transformative your recovery will be. The two of you may not always be at peace, but you can always be honest.

5. Break it down and track your progress

Trying to tackle the entire recovery process all at once can feel overwhelming and impossible. Instead, break your plan into smaller, more manageable steps and milestones. Celebrate each moment of progress or breakthrough, no matter how small. If you are stuck or discouraged, return to your plan and recommit to the next right action, one moment at a time.

Remember, your affair recovery plan is not meant to be a rigid, inflexible set of rules but rather a living, evolving framework for your healing journey. As you continue to grow and change, your plan can grow and change with you, adapting to new insights, challenges, and opportunities along the way.

The most important thing is to approach the process with intention, compassion, and a commitment to your healing and wholeness. Trust that, no matter how painful or uncertain things may feel in the moment, you have within you the strength, wisdom, and resilience to find your way through. And know that, with time, patience, and dedication, you can transform even the deepest wounds into opportunities for profound growth, connection, and love.

As Emma, a client who had been through her own difficult affair recovery journey, once shared with me: "Creating a plan was like building a bridge between the life I thought I had lost, and the one I knew was still possible. It allowed me to honor my pain and potential and stay anchored in my values even as I navigated the unknown. Looking back now, I can see how every step of that plan - even the ones that felt small or insignificant at the time - was an essential part of my healing and growth. It wasn't always easy, but it was always worth it."

So take heart, dear reader. The road ahead may be long and winding, but with a clear map and a courageous spirit, you can find your way to a brighter, more beautiful future - one step, one day, one moment at a time.

Reflection Questions:

1. What larger intentions or goals feel most important for you and your relationship in the affair recovery process? How can you use these to guide and anchor your more specific plans and actions?

2. What potential obstacles or triggers do you anticipate in your healing journey? What strategies or supports might help you navigate these more skillfully?

3. What rituals or practices can you build to nurture emotional and relational healing into your recovery plan? How can you prioritize these alongside more practical steps and agreements?

Reasons for Hope

As we come to the end of this journey together, I want to leave you with a message of hope and inspiration. Throughout these pages, we've explored the complex, painful, and often messy reality of affair recovery - the challenges and obstacles, the setbacks and breakthroughs, the moments of despair, and the glimmers of possibility. We've seen how, with commitment, compassion, and a willingness to grow, even the deepest wounds can become opportunities for transformation and renewal.

But I know that, during the struggle, it can be hard to hold onto hope. When you're in the thick of betrayal trauma, when trust has been shattered, and the future feels uncertain, it's easy to wonder if healing is truly possible. You might look at the wreckage of your relationship and question whether it can ever be rebuilt, whether you can ever find your way back to the love and connection you once shared.

Bear in mind that people only make changes when their old ways don't work anymore. At those times, they are willing to consider new ways of doing things and look at their situation through new eyes.

If you're in that place of struggle right now, I want to remind you of a simple but profound truth: you are not alone. The pain you are feeling, the doubts and fears, anger and grief—these are all normal, natural responses to the trauma of infidelity. They do not make you weak, broken, or unlovable. They make you human—a brave, resilient, feeling person who is facing one of life's greatest challenges with courage and heart.

And just as you are not alone in your pain, you are not alone in your potential for healing. Every day, countless couples find their way through the darkness of betrayal and back to the light of love and trust. They do the hard, vulnerable work of facing their wounds, telling the truth, forgiving, and recommitting. They learn and grow and discover new depths of strength and compassion within themselves and each other.

Take the story of Rachel and Eric. When Eric's affair came to light after 15 years of marriage, Rachel felt like her entire world had been shattered. The life she had built with the man she loved suddenly felt like an illusion, and she couldn't imagine how they would ever recover. For months, they cycled through intense emotions and painful, circular conversations, both wondering if it might be easier just to walk away. They wondered if ending their marriage or staying together was more painful.

But something in Rachel refused to give up on their love. Even in her anger and devastation, she could sense a deeper truth - that their relationship was worth fighting for, that the story of their marriage didn't have to end with betrayal. She committed herself to the hard work of healing, to showing up day after day with honesty, vulnerability, and a willingness to grow.

It wasn't easy, and there were many moments when Rachel doubted herself and the process. But slowly, with the help of a skilled therapist and their determination, she and Eric began to find their way back to each other. They learned to communicate from each of their hearts with greater clarity and empathy, to talk with each other in a healthy manner, to set healthy boundaries, to rebuild trust, and to reconnect with the love and commitment that had first brought them together.

As Rachel shared with me recently, "Our marriage today is not the same as it was before the affair - and honestly, I wouldn't want it to be. We've been through the fire together and emerged stronger, wiser, and more authentic. We've learned to love each other not in spite of our imperfections but because of them. While I wouldn't wish the pain of betrayal on anyone, I'm grateful for the growth and resilience it has brought us.

Or consider the journey of Marcus and Emily. When Emily discovered Marcus's infidelity, she was consumed by rage and despair. She couldn't eat, sleep, or imagine ever trusting him again. Marcus, drowning in shame and regret, didn't know how to begin to make amends.

For a long time, it seemed like their relationship might not survive the betrayal. They would have fleeting moments of connection and hope, only to be followed by explosive arguments that left them both feeling hopeless and alone. But through it all, they kept showing up - for each other, their children, and the love they knew was still alive beneath the pain.

With patience, determined practice, and the support of a caring therapist, Marcus and Emily slowly began to heal and rebuild. They learned to express their feelings without blame or defensiveness, take responsibility for their own choices and well-being, and forgive each other and themselves. They created new rituals of connection and intimacy and discovered a depth of love and resilience they never knew they had.

As Emily reflected recently, "The affair will always be a part of our story, but it no longer defines us. We've woven it into the larger tapestry of our marriage - the joys and sorrows, the laughter and tears, the moments of brokenness, and the moments of breakthrough. We've learned that healing isn't about returning to the way things were, but moving forward into a new, more honest, and wholehearted way of loving."

These stories, and countless others like them, prove that affair recovery is possible—that with commitment, compassion, and the right support, even the deepest wounds can heal. They remind us that the human heart is incredibly resilient and that we can all forgive, grow, and love again.

So, if you're feeling lost or hopeless right now or wondering how you'll ever find your way through this painful chapter - hold onto these stories as a lifeline. Let them remind you that you are not alone, that countless others have walked this path before you and emerged stronger and more loving on the other side.

And most importantly, hold onto your inner knowing - the quiet, unshakable voice that tells you that your love is worth fighting for, that your story isn't over yet. Trust that, with time, patience, and a willingness to grow, you can find your way back to wholeness and connection.

The journey of affair recovery is never easy, but it is always worthwhile. It asks us to confront our deepest fears and insecurities, to let go of our illusions of control and certainty, and to open our hearts to the unknown. It requires immense courage, vulnerability, and resilience - qualities that you might not always feel like you possess but are always within your reach.

While the path ahead may be long and winding, know that you do not walk it alone. You have an unshakable strength and wisdom within you; around you, you have a community of support and understanding. You have the love that first brought you together, the commitment that has sustained you through the years, and the hope that even now whispers new beginnings.

So take heart, dear reader. Keep putting one foot in front of the other and reaching for the light even when the darkness feels overwhelming. Keep choosing love, forgiveness, and growth, even when it's the hardest thing to do. And trust that, step by step, day by day, you are moving closer to the healed, whole, and loving relationship you desire and deserve. Recall that faith and fear originate from the same place. Do you have faith that things will improve or that things will worsen?

As the 13th-century poet Rumi once wrote, "The wound is the place where the light enters you." May you find the seeds of renewal and rebirth during your deepest pain and struggle. May you discover a stronger, wiser, and more beautiful love than you ever thought possible in the breaking open of your heart. May you come to know yourself as the brave, resilient, radiant being you truly are - capable of healing, loving, and creating the life and love your heart most longs for.

The journey is not over, but a new chapter is just beginning. With every step forward, you are claiming your power, potential, and profound capacity for transformation. You've got this, and I am cheering you on every step of the way.

With love and hope,

Jeff

About The Author

As a teenager, I experienced the devastation caused by infidelity first-hand when my family went through a parental affair. Navigating through the aftermath, which involved children's protective services, domestic abuse, legal fights, and emotional upheaval, left me feeling helpless and alone.

Determined to learn from these experiences, I became a Licensed Professional Counselor (LPC) and Licensed Chemical Dependency Counselor (LCDC). For over 40 years, I have helped thousands of families across various settings, applying an approach founded on proven Biblical principles and neuropsychology discoveries.

As an early pioneer in online counseling, I have been helping people through articles, e-books, and telephone sessions since 1999. My work has been featured on Wall Street Journal Radio, the Larry Elder Show, and numerous other media.

Married since 1985, my wife Peggy and I have been blessed with three incredible sons. We have navigated the challenges and temptations in our own marriage, and I am committed to helping others overcome the pain of affairs and rebuild their relationships.

You may contact me via email at jeff@restorethefamily.com.

Follow me on Medium @RestoreTheFamily

Receive my daily newsletter at www.SurviveYourPartnersAffair.com

The Affair Recovery Workhop

Transform Your Marriage

Are you ready to embark on a transformative journey to heal your marriage and rediscover the love, trust, and intimacy you once shared? The Affair Recovery Workshop, created by renowned relationship expert Jeffrey D. Murrah, LPC, LCDC, is your essential companion to this book, offering a unique and comprehensive approach to navigating the complex emotions and challenges that follow infidelity. With a proven track record of success and a personalized approach tailored to your needs, this workshop provides you with the in-depth guidance, interactive experience, and practical tools necessary to rebuild a stronger, more resilient relationship.

Why the Affair Recovery Workshop is the Essential Companion to this Book

1. In-depth Guidance: While the book lays a solid foundation for understanding infidelity and the recovery process, the video program dives deeper into the critical topics, offering 2.5 hours of expert guidance from Jeffrey D. Murrah. The extended format allows for a more thorough exploration of the strategies and techniques needed to rebuild trust, improve communication, and foster intimacy.

2. Interactive Experience: The video program provides an engaging and interactive learning experience that complements the book. With visual aids, real-life examples, and guided exercises, you can actively apply the concepts and strategies to your own situation, enhancing your understanding and retention of the material.

3. Personalized Approach: The Affair Recovery Workshop recognizes that every couple's situation is unique. The video program offers a personalized approach, helping you identify and address your relationship's specific challenges and dynamics. This targeted guidance can accelerate healing and lead to more effective outcomes.

4. Convenient and Flexible: With 24/7 access to the video modules, a comprehensive 68-page workbook, and a bonus ebook, "How Can I Trust You Again?", you can work through the program at your own pace, from the privacy and comfort of your own home. This flexibility ensures you can fully engage with the content and implement the strategies on your own terms.

Real Testimonials from Transformed Lives

"The Affair Recovery Workshop was the turning point in our healing journey. Jeffrey's in-depth guidance and personalized approach helped us navigate the complex emotions and rebuild our marriage stronger than ever." - Sarah and Michael, married 9 years.

"The interactive experience of the video program, combined with the practical exercises in the workbook, allowed us to dive deeper into understanding and addressing the unique challenges in our relationship. It was a game-changer for us." - Lisa and David, married 14 years.

Your Journey to a Stronger Marriage Starts Here

Invest in your marriage and your future happiness with the **Affair Recovery Workshop**. As a special offer exclusively available through this book, we're extending a 30% discount on the workshop to help you start your transformative journey. Visit **www.AffairRecoveryWorkshop.com** and use the coupon code **WORKSHOP30** to claim your discount. This limited-time offer is our commitment to your success.

Don't let infidelity define your marriage. Take the first step towards healing and renewal today, and give yourself the best opportunity to achieve the transformation you seek. With our 30-day unconditional guarantee, you have nothing to lose and everything to gain.

What You'll Receive:

- In-depth video modules (2.5 hours of expert guidance)
    - 68-page comprehensive workbook
    - Bonus ebook: "How Can I Trust You Again?"
    - 24/7 access to the program
    - 30-day unconditional guarantee
    - Strictly confidential participation

By combining the insights from the book with the immersive experience of the Affair Recovery Workshop, you'll be equipped with the knowledge, tools, and support needed to overcome the devastation of infidelity and build a stronger, more resilient marriage.

Take action now and claim your 30% discount on the Affair Recovery Workshop. Visit **www.AffairRecoveryWorkshop.com** and use the coupon code **WORKSHOP30** to start your transformative journey today. Your satisfaction is 100% guaranteed.

Wishing you all the best on your path to healing and rediscovering the love and connection you deserve,

Jeffrey D. Murrah, LPC, LCDC